ALSO BY SEAMUS HEANEY

POETRY

Death of a Naturalist

Door into the Dark

Wintering Out

North

Field Work

Poems 1965–1975

Sweeney Astray: A Version from the Irish

Station Island

The Haw Lantern

Selected Poems 1966–1987

Seeing Things

Sweeney's Flight *(with photographs by Rachel Giese)*

Laments by Jan Kochanowski
(translated with Stanisław Barańczak)

The Spirit Level

Opened Ground: Poems 1966–1996

Beowulf

Diary of One Who Vanished

Electric Light

District and Circle

The Testament of Cresseid and Seven Fables

The Rattle Bag *(edited with Ted Hughes)*

The School Bag *(edited with Ted Hughes)*

PROSE

Preoccupations: Selected Prose 1968–1978

The Government of the Tongue

The Redress of Poetry: Oxford Lectures

Finders Keepers: Selected Prose 1971–2001

PLAYS

The Cure at Troy: A Version of Sophocles' *Philoctetes*

The Burial at Thebes: A Version of Sophocles' *Antigone*

HUMAN CHAIN

HUMAN CHAIN

SEAMUS HEANEY

FARRAR, STRAUS AND GIROUX

NEW YORK

FARRAR, STRAUS AND GIROUX
18 West 18th Street, New York 10011

Printed in the United States of America
Originally published in 2010 by Faber and Faber Ltd, Great Britain
Published in the United States by Farrar, Straus and Giroux
First American edition, 2010

Some of these poems appeared for the first time in slightly different form in the
following magazines: *Agenda, Archipelago, Granta, Irish Pages, The Irish Times,
Little Star, Magenta, The New Republic, The New Yorker, Parnassus, Poetry Review,
The SHOp, The Times Literary Supplement.* "The Conway Stewart" and "'Lick the
pencil'" were first published in *Many Mansions* (Stoney Road Press, 2009); "Human
Chain" in *That Island Never Found: Essays and Poems for Terence Brown* (Four Courts
Press, 2007); "Slack" as a poem card and poster poem from Newcastle Centre
for the Literary Arts, 2009; "A Herbal" is a version of "Hebier de Bretagne" from
Guillevic's *Étier* (Gallimard, 1979) and appeared in *Franco-Irish Connections: Essays,
Memoirs and Poems in Honour of Pierre Joannon* (Four Courts Press, 2009); "The
Riverbank Field" and "Route 110" in *The Riverbank Field* (Gallery Press, 2007);
"Wraiths" in *From the Small Back Room: A Festschrift for Ciaran Carson* (Netherlea,
2008); "Parking Lot" appeared under the title "Wraiths" in *Captivating Brightness:
Ballynahinch* (Ballynahinch Castle Hotel/Occasional Press, 2008); "Hermit Songs"
in *Something Understood: Essays and Poetry for Helen Vendler* (University of Virginia
Press, 2009). "A Kite for Aibhín" is adapted from "The Kites," first published in
Auguri: To Mary Kelleher (Royal Dublin Society, 2009).

Library of Congress Cataloging-in-Publication Data
Heaney, Seamus, 1939–
Human Chain / Seamus Heaney. —1st American ed.
p.   cm.
ISBN 978-0-374-17351-7 (alk. paper)
I. Title

PR6058.E2H86 2010
821'.914—dc22

2010010274

Designed by Gretchen Achilles/Wavetrap Design

www.fsgbooks.com

1   3   5   7   9   10   8   6   4   2

FOR
DES AND MARY
PETER AND JEAN

CONTENTS

HUMAN CHAIN

"HAD I NOT BEEN AWAKE"

Had I not been awake I would have missed it,
A wind that rose and whirled until the roof
Pattered with quick leaves off the sycamore

And got me up, the whole of me a-patter,
Alive and ticking like an electric fence:
Had I not been awake I would have missed it,

It came and went so unexpectedly
And almost it seemed dangerously,
Returning like an animal to the house,

A courier blast that there and then
Lapsed ordinary. But not ever
After. And not now.

ALBUM

i

Now the oil-fired heating boiler comes to life
Abruptly, drowsily, like the timed collapse
Of a sawn-down tree, I imagine them

In summer season, as it must have been,
And the place, it dawns on me,
Could have been Grove Hill before the oaks were cut,

Where I'd often stand with them on airy Sundays
Shin-deep in hilltop bluebells, looking out
At Magherafelt's four spires in the distance.

Too late, alas, now for the apt quotation
About a love that's proved by steady gazing
Not at each other but in the same direction.

ii

Quercus, the oak. And *Quaerite*, Seek ye.
Among green leaves and acorns in mosaic
(Our college arms surmounted by *columba*,

Dove of the church, of Derry's sainted grove)
The footworn motto stayed indelible:
Seek ye first the Kingdom . . . Fair and square

I stood on in the Junior House hallway
A grey eye will look back
Seeing them as a couple, I now see,

For the first time, all the more together
For having had to turn and walk away, as close
In the leaving (or closer) as in the getting.

iii

It's winter at the seaside where they've gone
For the wedding meal. And I am at the table,
Uninvited, ineluctable.

A skirl of gulls. A smell of cooking fish.
Plump dormant silver. Stranded silence. Tears.
Their bibbed waitress unlids a clinking dish

And leaves them to it, under chandeliers.
And to all the anniversaries of this
They are not ever going to observe

Or mention even in the years to come.
And now the man who drove them here will drive
Them back, and by evening we'll be home.

iv

Were I to have embraced him anywhere
It would have been on the riverbank
That summer before college, him in his prime,

Me at the time not thinking how he must
Keep coming with me because I'd soon be leaving.
That should have been the first, but it didn't happen.

The second did, at New Ferry one night
When he was very drunk and needed help
To do up trouser buttons. And the third

Was on the landing during his last week,
Helping him to the bathroom, my right arm
Taking the webby weight of his underarm.

v

It took a grandson to do it properly,
To rush him in the armchair
With a snatch raid on his neck,

Proving him thus vulnerable to delight,
Coming as great proofs often come
Of a sudden, one-off, then the steady dawning

Of whatever *erat demonstrandum.*
Just as a moment back a son's three tries
At an embrace in Elysium

Swam up into my very arms, and in and out
Of the Latin stem itself, the phantom
Verus that has slipped from "very."

THE CONWAY STEWART

"Medium," 14-carat nib,
Three gold bands in the clip-on screw-top,
In the mottled barrel a spatulate, thin

Pump-action lever
The shopkeeper
Demonstrated,

The nib uncapped,
Treating it to its first deep snorkel
In a newly opened ink-bottle,

Guttery, snottery,
Letting it rest then at an angle
To ingest,

Giving us time
To look together and away
From our parting, due that evening,

To my longhand
"Dear"
To them, next day.

UNCOUPLED

i

Who is this coming to the ash-pit
Walking tall, as if in a procession,
Bearing in front of her a slender pan

Withdrawn just now from underneath
The firebox, weighty, full to the brim
With whitish dust and flakes still sparking hot

That the wind is blowing into her apron bib,
Into her mouth and eyes while she proceeds
Unwavering, keeping her burden horizontal still,

Hands in a tight, sore grip round the metal knob,
Proceeds until we have lost sight of her
Where the worn path turns behind the henhouse.

ii

Who is this, not much higher than the cattle,
Working his way towards me through the pen,
His ashplant in one hand

Lifted and pointing, a stick of keel
In the other, calling to where I'm perched
On top of a shaky gate,

Waving and calling something I cannot hear
With all the lowing and roaring, lorries revving
At the far end of the yard, the dealers

Shouting among themselves, and now to him
So that his eyes leave mine and I know
The pain of loss before I know the term.

THE BUTTS

His suits hung in the wardrobe, broad
And short
And slightly bandy-sleeved,

Flattened back
Against themselves,
A bit stand-offish.

Stale smoke and oxter-sweat
Came at you in a stirred-up brew
When you reached in,

A whole rake of thornproof and blue serge
Swung heavily
Like waterweed disturbed. I sniffed

Tonic unfreshness,
Then delved past flap and lining
For the forbidden handfuls.

But a kind of empty-handedness
Transpired . . . Out of suit-cloth
Pressed against my face,

Out of those layered stuffs
That surged and gave,
Out of the cold smooth pocket-lining

Nothing but chaff cocoons,
A paperiness not known again
Until the last days came

And we must learn to reach well in beneath
Each meagre armpit
To lift and sponge him,

One on either side,
Feeling his lightness,
Having to dab and work

Closer than anybody liked
But having, for all that,
To keep working.

CHANSON D'AVENTURE

Love's mysteries in souls do grow,
But yet the body is his book.

i

Strapped on, wheeled out, forklifted, locked
In position for the drive,
Bone-shaken, bumped at speed,

The nurse a passenger in front, you ensconced
In her vacated corner seat, me flat on my back—
Our postures all the journey still the same,

Everything and nothing spoken,
Our eyebeams threaded laser-fast, no transport
Ever like it until then, in the sunlit cold

Of a Sunday morning ambulance
When we might, O my love, have quoted Donne
On love on hold, body and soul apart.

ii

Apart: the very word is like a bell
That the sexton Malachy Boyle outrolled
In illo tempore in Bellaghy

Or the one I tolled in Derry in my turn
As college bellman, the haul of it there still
In the heel of my once capable

Warm hand, hand that I could not feel you lift
And lag in yours throughout that journey
When it lay flop-heavy as a bellpull

And we careered at speed through Dungloe,
Glendoan, our gaze ecstatic and bisected
By a hooked-up drip-feed to the cannula.

iii

The charioteer at Delphi holds his own,
His six horses and chariot gone,
His left hand lopped

From a wrist protruding like an open spout,
Bronze reins astream in his right, his gaze ahead
Empty as the space where the team should be,

His eyes-front, straight-backed posture like my own
Doing physio in the corridor, holding up
As if once more I'd found myself in step

Between two shafts, another's hand on mine,
Each slither of the share, each stone it hit
Registered like a pulse in the timbered grips.

MIRACLE

Not the one who takes up his bed and walks
But the ones who have known him all along
And carry him in—

Their shoulders numb, the ache and stoop deeplocked
In their backs, the stretcher handles
Slippery with sweat. And no let-up

Until he's strapped on tight, made tiltable
And raised to the tiled roof, then lowered for healing.
Be mindful of them as they stand and wait

For the burn of the paid-out ropes to cool,
Their slight lightheadedness and incredulity
To pass, those ones who had known him all along.

HUMAN CHAIN

FOR TERENCE BROWN

Seeing the bags of meal passed hand to hand
In close-up by the aid workers, and soldiers
Firing over the mob, I was braced again

With a grip on two sack corners,
Two packed wads of grain I'd worked to lugs
To give me purchase, ready for the heave—

The eye-to-eye, one-two, one-two upswing
On to the trailer, then the stoop and drag and drain
Of the next lift. Nothing surpassed

That quick unburdening, backbreak's truest payback,
A letting go which will not come again.
Or it will, once. And for all.

A MITE-BOX

But still in your cupped palm to feel
The chunk and clink of an alms-collecting mite-box,
Full to its slotted lid with copper coins,

Pennies and halfpennies donated for
"The foreign missions" . . . Made from a cardboard kit,
Wedge-roofed like a little oratory

And yours to tote as you made the rounds,
Indulged on every doorstep, each donation
Accounted for by a pinprick in a card—

A way for all to see a way to heaven,
The same as when a pinholed *camera
Obscura* unblinds the sun eclipsed.

AN OLD REFRAIN

i

Robin-run-the-hedge
We called the vetch—
A fading straggle

Of Lincoln green
English stitchwork
Unravelling

With a hey-nonny-no
Along the Wood Road.
Sticky entangling

Berry and thread
Summering in
On the tousled verge.

ii

In *seggins*
Hear the wind
Among the sedge,

In *boortree*
The elderberry's
Dank indulgence,

In *benweed*
Ragwort's
Singular unbending,

In *easing*
Drips of night rain
From the eaves.

THE WOOD ROAD

Resurfaced, never widened,
The verges grassy as when
Bill Pickering lay with his gun
Under the summer hedge
Nightwatching, in uniform—

Special militiaman.

Moonlight on rifle barrels,
On the windscreen of a van
Roadblocking the road,
The rest of his staunch patrol
In profile, sentry-loyal,

Harassing Mulhollandstown.

Or me in broad daylight
On top of a cartload
Of turf built trig and tight,
Looked up to, looking down,
Allowed the reins like an adult

As the old cart rocked and rollicked.

Then that August day I walked it
To the hunger striker's wake,
Across a silent yard,
In past a watching crowd
To where the guarded corpse

And a guard of honour stared.

Or the stain at the end of the lane
Where the child on her bike was hit
By a speed-merchant from nowhere
Hard-rounding the corner,
A back wheel spinning in sunshine,

A headlamp in smithereens.

Film it in sepia,
Drip-paint it in blood,
The Wood Road as is and was,
Resurfaced, never widened,
The milk-churn deck and the sign

For the bus-stop overgrown.

THE BALER

All day the clunk of a baler
Ongoing, cardiac-dull,
So taken for granted

It was evening before I came to
To what I was hearing
And missing: summer's richest hours

As they had been to begin with,
Fork-lifted, sweated-through
And nearly rewarded enough

By the giddied-up race of a tractor
At the end of the day
Last-lapping a hayfield.

But what I also remembered
As woodpigeons sued at the edge
Of thirty gleaned acres

And I stood inhaling the cool
In a dusk eldorado
Of mighty cylindrical bales

Was Derek Hill's saying,
The last time he sat at our table,
He could bear no longer to watch

The sun going down
And asking please to be put
With his back to the window.

DERRY DERRY DOWN

i

The lush
Sunset blush
On a big ripe

Gooseberry:
I scratched my hand
Reaching in

To gather it
Off the bush,
Unforbidden,

In Annie Devlin's
Overgrown
Back garden.

ii

In the storybook
Back kitchen
Of The Lodge

The full of a white
Enamel bucket
Of little pears:

Still life
On the red tiles
Of that floor.

Sleeping beauty
I came on
By the scullion's door.

EELWORKS

To win the hand of the princess
What tasks the youngest son
Had to perform!

For me, the first to come a-courting
In the fish factor's house,
It was to eat with them

An eel supper.

ii

Cut of diesel oil in evening air,
Tractor engines in the clinker-built
Deep-bellied boats,

Landlubbers' craft,
Heavy in water
As a cow down in a drain,

The men straight-backed,
Standing firm
At stern and bow—

Horse-and-cart men, really,
Glad when the adze-dressed keel
Cleaved to the mud.

Rum-and-peppermint men too
At the counter later on
In her father's pub.

iii

That skin Alfie Kirkwood wore
At school, sweaty-lustrous, supple

And bisected into tails
For the tying of itself around itself—

For strength, according to Alfie.
Who would ease his lapped wrist

From the flap-mouthed cuff
Of a jerkin rank with eel oil,

The abounding reek of it
Among our summer desks

My first encounter with the up close
That had to be put up with.

iv

Sweaty-lustrous too
The butt of the freckled
Elderberry shoot

I made a rod of,
A-fluster when I felt
Not tugging but a trailing

On the line, not the utter
Flip-stream frolic-fish
But a foot-long

Slither of a fellow,
A young eel, greasy grey
And rightly wriggle-spined,

Not yet the blueblack
Slick-backed waterwork
I'd live to reckon with,

My old familiar
Pearl-purl
Selkie-streaker.

v

"That tree," said Walter de la Mare
(Summer in his rare, recorded voice
So I could imagine

A lawn beyond French windows
And downs in the middle distance)
"That tree, saw it once

Struck by lightning . . . The bark—"
In his accent the *ba-aak*—
"The bark came off it

Like a girl taking off her petticoat."
White linen *éblouissante*
In a breath of air,

Sylph-flash made flesh,
Eelwork, sea-salt and dish cloth
Getting a first hold,

Then purchase for the thumbnail
And the thumb
Under a v-nick in the neck,

The skinpeel drawing down
Like silk
At a practised touch.

vi

On the hoarding and the signposts
"Lough Neagh Fishermen's Co-operative,"

But ever on our lips and at the weir
"The eelworks."

SLACK

i

Not coal dust, more the weighty grounds of coal
The lorryman would lug in open bags
And vent into a corner,

A sullen pile
But soft to the shovel, accommodating
As the clattering coal was not.

In days when life prepared for rainy days
It lay there, slumped and waiting
To dampen down and lengthen out

The fire, a check on mammon
And in its own way
Keeper of the flame.

ii

The sound it made
More to me
Than any allegory.

Slack schlock.
Scuttle scuffle.
Shak-shak.

And those words—
"Bank the fire"—
Every bit as solid as

The cindery skull
Formed when its tarry
Coral cooled.

iii

Out in the rain,
Sent out for it
Again

Stand in the unlit
Coalhouse door
And take in

Its violet blet,
Its wet sand weight,
Remembering it

Tipped and slushed
Catharsis
From the bag.

A HERBAL

AFTER GUILLEVIC'S "HERBIER DE BRETAGNE"

Everywhere plants
Flourish among graves,

Sinking their roots
In all the dynasties
Of the dead.

*

Was graveyard grass
In our place
Any different?

Different from ordinary
Field grass?

Remember how you wanted
The sound recordist
To make a loop,

Wildtrack of your feet
Through the wet
At the foot of a field?

*

Yet for all their lush
Compliant dialect
No way have plants here
Arrived at a settlement.

Not the mare's tail,
Not the broom or whins.

It must have to do
With the wind.

*

Not that the grass itself
Ever rests in peace.

It too takes issue,
Now sets its face

To the wind,
Now turns its back.

*

"See me?" it says.
"The wind

Has me well rehearsed
In the ways of the world.

Unstable is good.
Permission granted!

Go, then, citizen
Of the wind.
Go with the flow."

*

The bracken
Is less boastful.

It closes and curls back
On its secrets,

The best kept
Upon earth.

*

And, to be fair,
There is sun as well.

Nowhere else
Is there sun like here,

Morning sunshine
All day long.

Which is why the plants,
Even the bracken,

Are sometimes tempted
Into trust.

*

On sunlit tarmac,
On memories of the hearse

At walking pace
Between overgrown verges,

The dead here are borne
Towards the future.

*

When the funeral bell tolls
The grass is all a-tremble.

But only then.
Not every time any old bell

Rings.

*

Broom
Is like the disregarded
And company for them,

Shows them
They have to keep going,

That the whole thing's worth
The effort.

And sometimes
Like those same characters
When the weather's very good

Broom sings.

*

Never, in later days,
Would fruit

So taste of earth.
There was slate

In the blackberries,
A slatey sap.

*

Run your hand into
The ditchback growth

And you'd grope roots,
Thick and thin.
But roots of what?

Once, one that we saw
Gave itself away,

The tail of a rat
We killed.

*

We had enemies,
Though why we never knew.

Among them,
Nettles,

Malignant things, letting on
To be asleep.

*

Enemies—
Part of a world

Nobody seemed able to explain
But that had to be
Put up with.

There would always be dock leaves
To cure the vicious stings.

*

There were leaves on the trees
And growth on the headrigs

You could confess
Everything to.

Even your fears
Of the night,

Of people
Even.

*

What was better then

Than to crush a leaf or a herb
Between your palms,

Then wave it slowly, soothingly
Past your mouth and nose

And breathe?

*

If you know a bit
About the universe

It's because you've taken it in
Like that,

Looked as hard
As you look into yourself,

Into the rat hole,
Through the vetch and dock
That mantled it.

Because you've laid your cheek
Against the rush clump

And known soft stone to break
On the quarry floor.

*

Between heather and marigold,
Between sphagnum and buttercup,
Between dandelion and broom,
Between forget-me-not and honeysuckle,

As between clear blue and cloud,
Between haystack and sunset sky,
Between oak tree and slated roof,

I had my existence. I was there.
Me in place and the place in me.

*

Where can it be found again,
An elsewhere world, beyond

Maps and atlases,
Where all is woven into

And of itself, like a nest
Of crosshatched grass blades?

CANOPY

It was the month of May.
Trees in Harvard Yard
Were turning a young green.
There was whispering everywhere.

David Ward had installed
Voice-boxes in the branches,
Speakers wrapped in sacking
Looking like old wasps' nests

Or bat-fruit in the gloaming—
Shadow Adam's apples
That made sibilant ebb and flow,
Speech-gutterings, desultory

Hush and backwash and echo.
It was like a recording
Of antiphonal responses
In the congregation of leaves.

Or a wood that talked in its sleep.
Reeds on a riverbank
Going over and over their secret.
People were cocking their ears,

Gathering, quietening,
Stepping on to the grass,
Stopping and holding hands.
Earth was replaying its tapes,

Words being given new airs:
Dante's whispering wood—
The wood of the suicides—
Had been magicked to lovers' lane.

If a twig had been broken off there
It would have curled itself like a finger
Around the fingers that broke it
And then refused to let go

As if it were mistletoe
Taking tightening hold.
Or so I thought as the fairy
Lights in the boughs came on.

1994

THE RIVERBANK FIELD

Ask me to translate what Loeb gives as
"In a retired vale . . . a sequestered grove"
And I'll confound the Lethe in Moyola

By coming through Back Park down from Grove Hill
Across Long Rigs on to the riverbank—
Which way, by happy chance, will take me past

The *domos placidas*, "those peaceful homes"
Of Upper Broagh. Moths then on evening water
It would have to be, not bees in sunlight,

Midge veils instead of lily beds; but *stet*
To all the rest: the willow leaves
Elysian-silvered, the grass so fully fledged

And unimprinted it can't not conjure thoughts
Of passing spirit-troops, *animae, quibus altera fato*
Corpora debentur, "spirits," that is,

"To whom second bodies are owed by fate."
And now to continue, as enjoined to often,
"In my own words":

"All these presences
Once they have rolled time's wheel a thousand years
Are summoned here to drink the river water

So that memories of this underworld are shed
And soul is longing to dwell in flesh and blood
Under the dome of the sky."

AFTER *AENEID VI*, 704–715 & 748–751

ROUTE 110

i

In a stained front-buttoned shopcoat—
Sere brown piped with crimson—
Out of the Classics bay into an aisle

Smelling of dry rot and disinfectant
She emerges, absorbed in her coin-count,
Eyes front, right hand at work

In the slack marsupial vent
Of her change-pocket, thinking what to charge
For a used copy of *Aeneid VI.*

Dustbreath bestirred in the cubicle mouth
I inhaled as she slid my purchase
Into a deckle-edged brown paper bag.

ii

Smithfield Market Saturdays. The pet shop
Fetid with droppings in the rabbit cages,
Melodious with canaries, green and gold,

But silent now as birdless Lake Avernus.
I hurried on, shortcutting to the buses,
Parrying the crush with my bagged Virgil,

Past booths and the jambs of booths with their displays
Of canvas schoolbags, maps, prints, plaster plaques,
Feather dusters, artificial flowers,

Then racks of suits and overcoats that swayed
When one was tugged from its overcrowded frame
Like their owners' shades close-packed on Charon's barge.

iii

Once the driver wound a little handle
The destination names began to roll
Fast-forward in their panel, and everything

Came to life. Passengers
Flocked to the kerb like agitated rooks
Around a rookery, all go

But undecided. At which point the inspector
Who ruled the roost in bus station and bus
Separated and directed everybody

By calling not the names but the route numbers,
And so we scattered as instructed, me
For Route 110, Cookstown via Toome and Magherafelt.

iv

Tarpaulin-stiff, coal-black, sharp-cuffed as slate,
The standard-issue railway guard's long coat
I bought once second-hand: suffering its scourge

At the neck and wrists was worth it even so
For the dismay I caused by doorstep night arrivals,
A creature of cold blasts and flap-winged rain.

And then, come finer weather, up and away
To Italy, in a wedding guest's bargain suit
Of finest weave, loose-fitting, summery, grey

As Venus' doves, hotfooting it with the tanned expats
Up their Etruscan slopes to a small brick chapel
To find myself the one there most at home.

v

Venus' doves? Why not McNicholls' pigeons
Out of their pigeon holes but homing still?
They lead unerringly to McNicholls' kitchen

And a votive jampot on the dresser shelf.
So reach me not a gentian but stalks
From the bunch that stood in it, each head of oats

A silvered smattering, each individual grain
Wrapped in a second husk of glittering foil
They'd saved from chocolate bars, then pinched and cinched

"To give the wee altar a bit of shine."
The night old Mrs. Nick, as she was to us,
Handed me one it as good as lit me home.

vi

It was the age of ghosts. Of hand-held flashlamps.
Lights moving at a distance scried for who
And why: whose wake, say, in which house on the road

In that direction—Michael Mulholland's the first
I attended as a full participant,
Sitting up until the family rose

Like strangers to themselves and us. A wake
Without the corpse of their own dear ill-advised
Sonbrother swimmer, lost in the Bristol Channel.

For three nights we kept conversation going
Around the waiting trestles. By the fourth
His coffin, with the lid on, was in place.

vii

The corpse house then a house of hospitalities
Right through the small hours, the ongoing card game
Interrupted constantly by rounds

Of cigarettes on plates, biscuits, cups of tea,
The antiphonal recital of known events
And others rare, clandestine, undertoned.

Apt pupil in their night school, I walked home
On the last morning, my clothes as smoke-imbued
As if I'd fed a pyre, accompanied to the gable

By the mother, to point out a right of way
Across their fields, into our own back lane,
And absolve me thus formally of trespass.

viii

As one when the month is young sees a new moon
Fading into daytime, again it is her face
At the dormer window, her hurt still new,

My look behind me hurried as I unlock,
Switch on, rev up, pull out and drive away
In the car she'll not have taken her eyes off,

The brakelights flicker-flushing at the corner
Like red lamps swung by RUC patrols
In the small hours on pre-Troubles roads

After dances, after our holdings on
And holdings back, the necking
And nay-saying age of impurity.

And what in the end was there left to bury
Of Mr. Lavery, blown up in his own pub
As he bore the primed device and bears it still

Mid-morning towards the sun-admitting door
Of Ashley House? Or of Louis O'Neill
In the wrong place the Wednesday they buried

Thirteen who'd been shot in Derry? Or of bodies
Unglorified, accounted for and bagged
Behind the grief cordons: not to be laid

In war graves with full honours, nor in a separate plot
Fired over on anniversaries
By units drilled and spruce and unreconciled.

x

Virgil's happy shades in pure blanched raiment
Contend on their green meadows, while Orpheus
Weaves among them, sweeping strings, aswerve

To the pulse of his own playing and to avoid
The wrestlers, dancers, runners on the grass.
Not unlike a sports day in Bellaghy,

Slim Whitman's wavering tenor amplified
Above sparking dodgems, flying chair-o-planes,
A mile of road with parked cars in the twilight

And teams of grown men stripped for action
Going hell for leather until the final whistle,
Leaving stud-scrapes on the pitch and on each other.

xi

Those evenings when we'd just wait and watch
And fish. Then the evening the otter's head
Appeared in the flow, or was it only

A surface-ruck and gleam we took for
An otter's head? No doubting, all the same,
The gleam, a turnover warp in the black

Quick water. Or doubting the solid ground
Of the riverbank field, twilit and a-hover
With midge-drifts, as if we had commingled

Among shades and shadows stirring on the brink
And stood there waiting, watching,
Needy and ever needier for translation.

xii

And now the age of births. As when once
At dawn from the foot of our back garden
The last to leave came with fresh-plucked flowers

To quell whatever smells of drink and smoke
Would linger on where mother and child were due
Later that morning from the nursing home,

So now, as a thank-offering for one
Whose long wait on the shaded bank has ended,
I arrive with my bunch of stalks and silvered heads

Like tapers that won't dim
As her earthlight breaks and we gather round
Talking baby talk.

DEATH OF A PAINTER

IN MEMORY OF NANCY WYNNE-JONES

Not a tent of blue but a peek of gold
From her coign of vantage in the studio,
A Wicklow cornfield in the gable window.

Long gazing at the hill—but not Cézanne,
More Thomas Hardy working to the end
In his crocheted old heirloom of a shawl.

And now not Hardy but a butterfly,
One of the multitude he imagined airborne
Through Casterbridge, down the summer thoroughfare.

And now not a butterfly but Jonah entering
The whale's mouth, as the Old English says,
Like a mote through a minster door.

LOUGHANURE

IN MEMORY OF COLIN MIDDLETON

i

Smoke might have been already in his eyes
The way he'd narrow them to size you up
As if you were a canvas, all the while

Licking and sealing a hand-rolled cigarette,
Each small ash increment flicked off
As white as flecks on the horizon line

Of his painting of Loughanure, thirty guineas
Forty-odd years ago. Whitewashed gables
Like petals stripped from hawthorn, heather ground

A pother of Gaeltacht turf smoke. Every time
He came to the house, he would go and stand
Gazing at it, grunting a bit and nodding.

ii

So this is what an afterlife can come to?
A cloud-boil of grey weather on the wall
Like murky crystal, a remembered stare—

This for an answer to Alighieri
And Plato's Er? Who watched immortal souls
Choose lives to come according as they were

Fulfilled or repelled by existences they'd known
Or suffered first time round. Saw great far-seeing
Odysseus in the end choose for himself

The destiny of a private man. Saw Orpheus
Because he'd perished at the women's hands
Choose rebirth as a swan.

iii

And did I seek the Kingdom? Will the Kingdom
Come? The idea of it there,
Behind its scrim since font and fontanel,

Breaks like light or water,
Like giddiness I felt at the old story
Of how he'd turn away from the motif,

Spread his legs, bend low, then look between them
For the mystery of the hard and fast
To be unveiled, his inverted face contorting

Like an arse-kisser's in some vision of the damned
Until he'd straighten, turn back, cock an eye
And stand with the brush at arm's length, readying.

iv

Had I had sufficient Irish in Rannafast
In 1953 to understand
The *seanchas* and *dinnsheanchas,*

Had not been too young and too shy,
Had even heard the story about Caoilte
Hunting the fawn from Tory to a door

In a fairy hill where he wasn't turned away
But led to a crystal chair on the hill floor
While a girl with golden ringlets harped and sang,

Language and longing might have made a leap
Up through that cloud-swabbed air, the horizon lightened
And the far "Lake of the Yew Tree" gleamed.

v

Not all that far, as it turns out,
Now that I can cover those few miles
In almost as few minutes, Mount Errigal

On the skyline the one constant thing
As I drive unhomesick, unbelieving, through
A grant-aided, renovated scene, trying

To remember the Greek word signifying
A world restored completely: that would include
Hannah Mhór's turkey-chortle of Irish,

The swan at evening over *Loch an Iubhair*,
Clarnico Murray's hard iced caramels
A penny an ounce over Sharkey's counter.

WRAITHS

FOR CIARAN CARSON

i *SIDHE*

She took me into the ground, the spade-marked
Clean-cut inside of a dugout
Meant for calves.

Dung on the floor, a damp gleam
And seam of sand like white gold
In the earth wall, nicked fibres in the roof.

We stood under the hill, out of the day
But faced towards the daylight, holding hands,
Inhaling the excavated bank.

Zoom in over our shoulders,
A tunnelling shot that accelerates and flares.
Discover us against weird brightness. Cut.

ii PARKING LOT

We were wraiths in the afternoon.
The bus had stopped. There was neither waiting room
Nor booth nor bench, only a parking lot

Above the town, open as a hillfort,
A panned sky and a light wind blowing.
We were on our way to the Gaeltacht,

Between languages, half in thrall to desire,
Half shy of it, when a flit of the foreknown
Blinked off a sunlit lake near the horizon

And passed into us, climbing and clunking up
Those fretted metal steps, as we reboarded
And were reincarnated seat by seat.

iii   WHITE NIGHTS

Furrow-plodders in spats and bright clasped brogues
Are cradling bags and hoisting beribboned drones
As their skilled neck-pullers' fingers force the chanters

And the whole band starts rehearsing
Its stupendous, swaggering march
Inside the hall. Meanwhile

One twilit field and summer hedge away
We wait for the learner who will stay behind
Piping by stops and starts,

Making an injured music for us alone,
Early-to-beds, white-night absentees
Open-eared to this day.

SWEENEY OUT-TAKES

FOR GREGORY OF CORKUS

i OTTERBOY

"Eorann writes with news of our two otters
Courting yesterday morning by the turnhole.
I can see them at their shiny romps

And imagine myself an otterboy
Kneeling where Ronan stands in cleric's vestment,
His hand outstretched to turn the bordered page

Of a massbook I hold high for his perusal,
My brow inclined to those big thong-tied feet
Protruding from the alb. Then shake myself

Like a waterdog that bounds out on the bank
To drop whatever he's retrieved and gambol
In pelt-sluice and unruly riverbreath."

ii HE REMEMBERS LYNCHECHAUN

"That three-leggèd, round-bellied, cast-iron pot
Deep in the nettle clump, cobweb-mouthed
And black-frost cold

After its cauldron life of plump and boil,
Reminds me of the cool consideration
Behind the busy warmth

Of Lynchechaun; and its heaviness
When I'd lift it off the crane,
Its lightening once I'd tilt and drain it

I now see as premonitions
Of my seeing through him, the dizziness
As scales fell from my eyes."

iii   THE PATTERN

"Full face, foursquare, eyelevel, carved in stone,
An ecclesiastic on the low-set lintel
Vested and unavoidable as the one

I approached head-on the full length of an aisle—
Unready as I was if much rehearsed
In the art of first confession.

What transpired next was meltwater,
A little trickle on the patterned tiles,
Truthfunk and walkaway, but then

In the nick of time, heelturn, comeback
And a clean breast made
Manfully if late. The pattern set."

COLUM CILLE CECINIT

i IS SCÍTH MO CHROB ÓN SCRÍBAINN

My hand is cramped from penwork.
My quill has a tapered point.
Its bird-mouth issues a blue-dark
Beetle-sparkle of ink.

Wisdom keeps welling in streams
From my fine-drawn sallow hand:
Riverrun on the vellum
Of ink from green-skinned holly.

My small runny pen keeps going
Through books, through thick and thin,
To enrich the scholars' holdings—
Penwork that cramps my hand.

ii IS AIRE CHARAIM DOIRE

Derry I cherish ever.
It is calm, it is clear.
Crowds of white angels on their rounds
At every corner.

iii *FIL SÚIL NGLAIS*

Towards Ireland a grey eye
Will look back but not see
Ever again
The men of Ireland or her women.

11TH/12TH CENTURY

HERMIT SONGS

FOR HELEN VENDLER

Above the ruled quires of my book
I hear the wild birds jubilant.

i

With cut-offs of black calico,
Remnants of old blackout blinds
Ironed, tacked with criss-cross threads,
We jacketed the issued books.

Less durable if more desired,
The mealy textured wallpaper:
Its brede of bosomed roses pressed
And flattened under smoothing irons.

Brown parcel paper, if need be.
Newsprint, even. Anything
To make a covert for the newness,
Learn you were a keeper only.

ii

Open, settle, smell, begin.
A spelling out, a finger trace:
One with Fursa, Colmcille,
The riddle-solving anchorites—

Macóige of Lismore, for instance,
Who, when asked which attribute
Of character was best, replied
"Steadiness, for it is best

When a man has set his hand to tasks
To persevere. I have never heard
Fault found with that." Tongue-tried words
Finger-traced, retraced, lip-read.

iii

Bread and pencils. Musty satchel.
The age of lessons to be learnt.
Reader, ours were "reading books"
And we were "scholars," our good luck

To get such schooling in the first place
For all its second and third handings.
The herdsman by the roadside told you.
The sibyls of the chimney corner.

The age of wonders too, such as:
Rubbings out with balls of bread-pith,
Birds and butterflies in "transfers"
Like stamps from Eden on a flyleaf.

iv

The master's store an otherwhere:
Penshafts sheathed in black tin—was it?—
A metal wrap, at any rate,
A tight nib-holding cuticle—

And nibs in packets by the gross,
Powdered ink, bunched cedar pencils,
Jotters, exercise books, rulers
Stacked like grave goods on the shelves.

The privilege of being sent
To fetch a box of pristine chalk
Or perfect copperplate examples
Of headline script for copying out.

v

"There are three right ways to spell *tu*.
Can you tell me how you write that down?"
The herdsman asks. And when we can't,
"Ask the master if *he* can."

Neque, Caesar says, *fas esse
existimant ea litteris
mandare.* "Nor do they think it right
To commit the things they know to writing."

Not, that is, until there comes
The psalm book called in Irish *cathach*,
Meaning "battler," meaning victory
When borne three times round an army.

vi

Sparks the Ulster warriors struck
Off wielded swords made Bricriu's hall
Blaze like the sun, according to
The Dun Cow scribe; and then Cuchulain

Entertained the embroidery women
By flinging needles in the air
So as they fell the point of one
Partnered with the eye of the next

To form a glittering reeling chain—
As in my dream a gross of nibs
Spills off the shelf, airlifts and links
Into a giddy gilt corona.

vii

A vision of the school the school
Won't understand, nor I, not quite:
My hand in the cold of a running stream
Suspended, a glass beaker dipped

And filling in the flow. I'm sent,
The privileged one, for water
To turn ink powder into ink—
Out in the open, the land and sky

And playground silent, a singing class
I've been excused from going on,
Coming out through opened windows,
Yet still and all a world away.

viii

"Inkwell" now as robbed of sense
As "inkhorn": a dun cow's, perhaps,
Stuck upside down at dipping distance
In the floor of the cell. Hence Colmcille's

Extempore when a loudmouth lands
Breaking the Iona silence:
This harbour shouter (it roughly goes),
Staff in hand, he will come along

Inclined to kiss the kiss of peace,
He will blunder in,
His toe will catch and overturn
My little inkhorn, spill my ink.

ix

A great one has put faith in "meaning"
That runs through space like a word
Screaming and protesting, another in
"Poet's imaginings

And memories of love":
Mine for now I put
In steady-handedness maintained
In books against its vanishing.

Books of Lismore. Kells. Armagh.
Of Lecan, its great Yellow Book.
"The battler," berry-browned, enshrined.
The cured hides. The much tried pens.

"LICK THE PENCIL"

i

"Lick the pencil" we might have called him
So quick he was to wet the lead, so deft
His hand-to-mouth and tongue-flirt round the stub.

Or "Drench the cow," so fierce his nostril-grab
And peel-back of her lip, so accurately forced
The bottle-neck between her big bare teeth.

Or "Catch the horse," for in spite of the low-set
Cut of him, he could always slip an arm
Around the neck and fit winkers on

In a single move. But as much for the surprise
As for the truth of it, "Lick the pencil"
Is what it's going to be.

ii

A "copying pencil," so called who knows why,
That inked itself and purpled when you licked,
About as short

As the cigarette butts in his pocket
And every bit as tangy, in constant need
Of sharpening, then of testing

On the back of his left hand, the line as bright
As bloodlines holly leaves might score
On the back of a bird-nester's,

Indelible as the glum grey pocks
White dandelion milk
Would mark your skin with as it dried.

iii

In memory of him, behold those pigmentations
Moisten and magnify to resemble marks
On Colmcille's monk's habit

The day he died, the day he didn't need
To catch the horse since the horse had come to him
Where he sat beside a path

Because, as the *Vita* says, "he was weary."
And the horse "wept on his breast
So the saint's clothes were made wet."

Then "Let him, Diarmait, be," said Colmcille
To his attendant, "till he has sorrowed for me
And cried his fill."

"THE DOOR WAS OPEN AND
THE HOUSE WAS DARK"

IN MEMORY OF DAVID HAMMOND

The door was open and the house was dark
Wherefore I called his name, although I knew
The answer this time would be silence

That kept me standing listening while it grew
Backwards and down and out into the street
Where as I'd entered (I remember now)

The streetlamps too were out.
I felt, for the first time there and then, a stranger,
Intruder almost, wanting to take flight

Yet well aware that here there was no danger,
Only withdrawal, a not unwelcoming
Emptiness, as in a midnight hangar

On an overgrown airfield in late summer.

IN THE ATTIC

i

Like Jim Hawkins aloft in the cross-trees
Of *Hispaniola*, nothing underneath him
But still green water and clean bottom sand,

The ship aground, the canted mast far out
Above a sea-floor where striped fish pass in shoals—
And when they've passed, the face of Israel Hands

That rose in the shrouds before Jim shot him dead
Appears to rise again . . . "But he was dead enough,"
The story says, "being both shot and drowned."

ii

A birch tree planted twenty years ago
Comes between the Irish Sea and me
At the attic skylight, a man marooned

In his own loft, a boy
Shipshaped in the crow's nest of a life,
Airbrushed to and fro, wind-drunk, braced

By all that's thrumming up from keel to masthead,
Rubbing his eyes to believe them and this most
Buoyant, billowy, topgallant birch.

iii

Ghost-footing what was then the *terra firma*
Of hallway linoleum, Grandfather now appears,
His voice a-waver like the draught-prone screen

They'd set up in the Club Rooms earlier
For the matinee I've just come back from.
"And Isaac Hands," he asks. "Was Isaac in it?"

His memory of the name a-waver too,
His mistake perpetual, once and for all,
Like the single splash when Israel's body fell.

iv

As I age and blank on names,
As my uncertainty on stairs
Is more and more the lightheadedness

Of a cabin boy's first time on the rigging,
As the memorable bottoms out
Into the irretrievable,

It's not that I can't imagine still
That slight untoward rupture and world-tilt
As a wind freshened and the anchor weighed.

A KITE FOR AIBHÍN

AFTER "L'AQUILONE" BY GIOVANNI PASCOLI (1855-1912)

Air from another life and time and place,
Pale blue heavenly air is supporting
A white wing beating high against the breeze,

And yes, it is a kite! As when one afternoon
All of us there trooped out
Among the briar hedges and stripped thorn,

I take my stand again, halt opposite
Anahorish Hill to scan the blue,
Back in that field to launch our long-tailed comet.

And now it hovers, tugs, veers, dives askew,
Lifts itself, goes with the wind until
It rises to loud cheers from us below.

Rises, and my hand is like a spindle
Unspooling, the kite a thin-stemmed flower
Climbing and carrying, carrying farther, higher

The longing in the breast and planted feet
And gazing face and heart of the kite flier
Until string breaks and—separate, elate—

The kite takes off, itself alone, a windfall.